A New True Book

SCIENCE EXPERIMENTS

By Vera R. Webster

This "true book" was prepared
under the direction of
Illa Podendorf,
formerly with the Laboratory School,
University of Chicago

CHILDRENS PRESS, CHICAGO

Magnets attract objects made
of iron or steel.

PHOTO CREDITS

Tony Freeman—Cover, 2, 4 (3 photos), 6, 7, 9, 12,
13, 16 (2 photos), 17, 20 (2 photos), 21 (2 photos),
23 (2 photos), 24, 25, 26, 27, 29, 30, 34, (2 photos),
36 (left), 38 (2 photos), 40 (2 photos), 41, 42, 43,
(2 photos)

Abbott Hunsucker—10, 14, 15, 18

Inland Steel Co.—31

Jim Berryman—33 (bottom)

Lynn Stone—33 (top)

James Mejuto—36 (middle and right)

Tom Winter—37

COVER—Experimenting with a magnet

Library of Congress Cataloging in Publication Data

Webster, Vera R.
  Science experiments.

  (A New true book)
  Includes index.
  Summary: Includes brief discussions
and experiments about force and motions, gravity,
magnets, energy and motion, wheels, pulleys,
and gears.
    1. Science—Experiments—Juvenile literature.
[1. Science—Experiments. 2. Experiments]
I. Title.
Q164.W43   530'.07'8   82-4429
ISBN 0-516-01646-6   AACR2

TABLE OF CONTENTS

FORCE AND MOTION

A jet plane flies overhead.

An automobile rolls along a highway.

A fan spins around and around.

A boy jogs along the street.

All of these things are moving.

What makes them move?

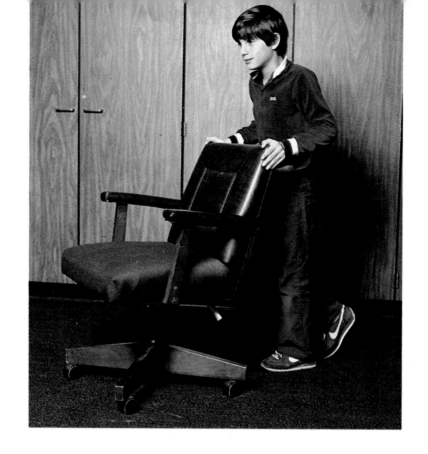

Things do not start to move by themselves.

Move a chair. What did you do to make it move?

Did you push it or pull it?

Things need a push or a
pull to make them move.
Pushes and pulls are
called forces.

WHICH WAY
DOES IT GO?

Roll a ball across the floor. Did you push it or pull it? Did the ball roll in the same direction as your push?

Drag a box across the room. Did you push it or pull it? Did the box move in the same direction as your pull?

A push or a pull is
needed to start something
moving. The thing will
move in the direction of
the push or the pull.

It takes
force to
pull a wagon.

HOW MUCH FORCE
IS NEEDED?

Forces may be different.
A large force may be
used to move a big thing.
A small force may be used
to move a small thing.
Try it and see.

EXPERIMENT

Tie a string around a wooden block. Then tie the string to a heavy rubber band. Pull the block. What happens?

Now put a string around a brick. Then tie the string to the rubber band. Pull the brick.

Which was harder to pull? Which needed more force? How could you tell?

WHEN FORCES ARE EQUAL

One boy pushes a desk in one direction. Another boy pushes in the opposite direction. One boy pushes just as hard as the other. The forces are the same. Will the desk move?

If one boy pushes harder than the other, will the desk move? In which direction will it move? Try it and see.

TUG-OF-WAR

When pulls are the same
from both sides, then a
thing will not move.

If one pull is bigger in
one direction, then a thing
will move. Which way will
it move?

A PULLING FORCE

Gravity is the pull of the earth.

Sleds slide downhill because of the pull of gravity.

Water runs downhill
because of the pull of
gravity.

Things fall to the earth
because of the pull of
gravity.

When you jump up, you always come down. Gravity pulls you down.

When you throw a ball up, it always comes down. Gravity pulls it down.

How hard does gravity pull?

EXPERIMENT

Feel the pull of gravity.

Hold a book in your hand and extend your arm outward.

Can you feel your arm getting tired? Gravity is pulling down on it. Don't drop the book.

MEASURING THE PULL OF GRAVITY

When you weigh yourself, you are measuring the pull of gravity.

Weigh some things. Weight is a measure of gravity. The heavier the thing is, the greater is the pull of gravity.

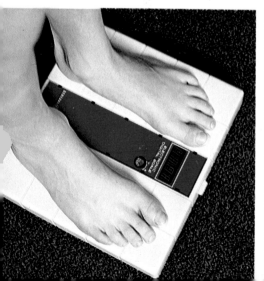

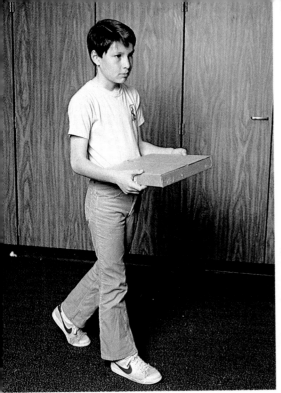 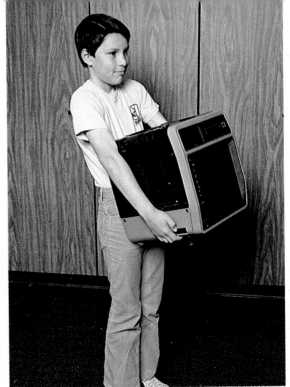

When you lift something, your pull is opposite to the pull of gravity. Try lifting different things—heavy things and light things.

Does gravity pull harder on light things or heavy things?

The pull of gravity holds
things on the earth—
buildings, automobiles,
trains, and even you. What
must we do to get off the
earth?

Airplanes and cranes are
strong enough to overcome
the pull of gravity.

A force opposite to the
pull of gravity lifts things
off the earth.

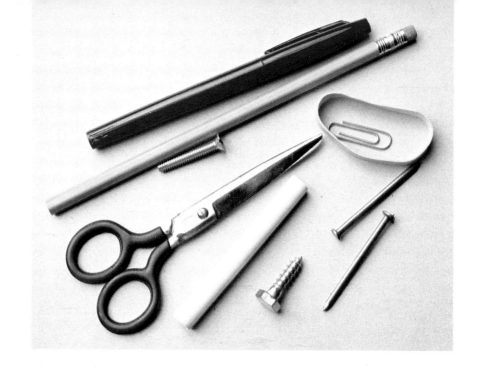

MAGNETS

Use a magnet to pick up some things. Do you know which of these things a magnet will pick up?

A magnet will pick up
none of these things.

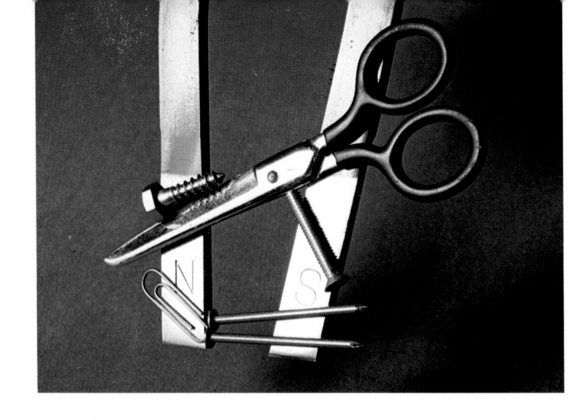

A magnet will pick up
all of these things. These
things are made of iron
and steel.

Magnets will pick up
things made of iron or
steel.

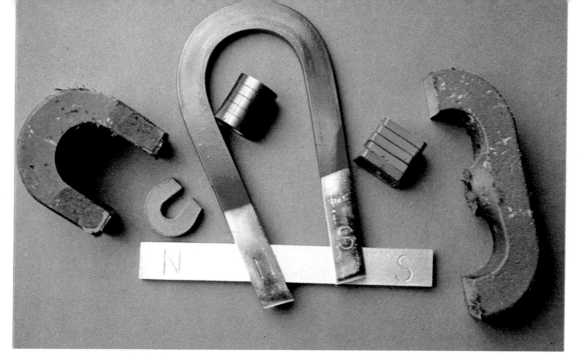

Magnets come in different shapes. They come in different sizes.

Big magnets are not always the strongest.

You can find out some interesting things about magnets. Turn to the next page.

MAGNETIC POLES

The ends of magnets are called poles. A magnet has a north-seeking pole and a south-seeking pole.

Can you find out which is which?

EXPERIMENT

Use two bar magnets.

Hang one bar magnet so that it swings free. When the magnet stops swinging, mark the end that points north with an "N." Mark the end that points south with an "S."

Now do the same thing with the other bar magnet.

Why do you think the magnet points north and south?

ANOTHER EXPERIMENT

Now use the magnets marked "N" and "S." Let one hang from the string. Then hold the "N" pole next to the other "N" pole. What happens?

Now hold the "S" pole next to the other "S" pole. What happens?

Now hold an "S" pole next to an "N" pole. What happens?

A giant
electromagnet
at work at a
steel plant

You will discover that two like poles push away from each other. Two unlike poles will pull together.

The way magnets push and pull make them very useful.

ENERGY AND MOTION

Energy is used whenever something is made to move. Energy is needed to push or pull. Energy in one form can be changed into another form.

Energy from falling water can be changed into electric energy.

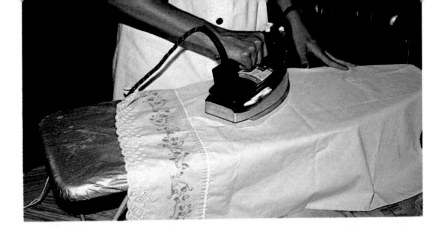

Electric energy can be changed into heat in an iron, into light in a lamp, and into mechanical energy (motion) in a fan.

Wind is moving air.
Energy in moving air can
be used to move other
things—windmills, sailboats,
and balloons.

MAKE A WINDMILL

Cut a 5-inch (12.7 centimeter) square from a sheet of paper. Cut along diagonal lines nearly to the center, as shown in the diagram.

Put a pin through 1, 2, 3, and 4 and then through the center of the square.

Stick pin into the eraser end on a pencil.

Run with the pencil in your hand. Does your windmill turn? If the wind is blowing, do you need to run? Try it and see.

When you push or pull,
you use energy. Where
does your energy come
from?

Food gives you energy
to move. It gives you
energy to push or pull.

When a push or pull moves something, it is called work.

Energy is always needed to do work.

Automobiles, trains, and planes get their energy from fuels.

WHEELS MAKE WORK EASIER

Look at the two garbage cans shown in the pictures. Which can is easier to move?

Try it and see.

EXPERIMENT

Use a pair of roller skates.

Fasten a rubber band to each skate.

Hold one of the rubber bands and pull one skate with it lying on its side.

Hold the other rubber band and pull the skate on its wheels.

Which skate needs the most pull?

How can you tell?

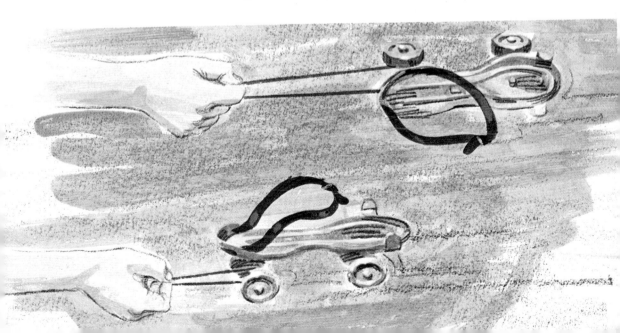

PULLEYS

Wheels help to lift things.

Wheels to lift things are called pulleys.

Can you find the pulleys in these pictures?

The more pulleys that are used, the easier it is to lift something.

GEARS

A wheel with teeth is called a gear.

Gear wheels can be used to turn other wheels. Gears are used in clocks, windup toys, and in automobiles.

Eggbeaters use gears
to turn the blades. Do the
activity on the next page
to learn about gears.

ACTIVITY

Borrow a rotary eggbeater. Examine it carefully. Then try it out.

Can you tell which wheel moves fastest? Do all the wheels turn in the same direction? What happens when you turn the handle?

Try it and see.

WORDS YOU SHOULD KNOW

activity(ak • TIV • ih • tee) — something to do; lesson

diagonal(dye • AG • un • il) slanting downward from one corner to another

diagram(DYE • ah • gram) — a drawing that shows how something works

energy(EN • er • gee) — the ability to do work; power

extend(ex • TEND) — to reach out

fasten(FASS • en) — to attach

force(FORSS) — strength; power; energy

gear(GEER) — a wheel with teeth around the edge

gravity(GRAV • ih • tee) — the force by which the earth pulls objects toward its center

mechanical(meh • KAN • ih • kul) — having to do with machines

opposite(OP • uh • zit) — completely different; move away from each other

pulley(PULL • ee) — a type of simple machine used to move heavy loads

rotary(ROH • tuh • ree) — to turn around on a center point

seek — look for; search

unlike — different; not the same

INDEX

About the Author

Vera Webster is widely recognized in the publishing field as an editor and author of science and environmental materials for both the juvenile and adult readers. She has conducted numerous educational seminars and workshops to provide teachers and parents with opportunities to learn more about children and their learning process. A North Carolina resident and mother of two grown daughters, Mrs. Webster is the president of Creative Resource Systems, Inc.